Make It Healthy

Lisa Greathouse

Consultant

Gina Montefusco, RN
Children's Hospital Los Angeles
Los Angeles, California

Publishing Credits

Dona Herweck Rice, *Editor-in-Chief*
Lee Aucoin, *Creative Director*
Don Tran, *Print Production Manager*
Timothy J. Bradley, *Illustration Manager*
Chris McIntyre, M.A.Ed., *Editorial Director*
James Anderson, M.S.Ed., *Editor*
Stephanie Reid, *Photo Editor*
Rachelle Cracchiolo, M.S.Ed., *Publisher*

Image Credits

Cover Wavebreakmedia ltd/Shutterstock; p.1 Wavebreakmedia ltd/Shutterstock; p.4(left) Sarsmis/Shutterstock; p.4(right) Tischenko Irina/Shutterstock; p.5(middle) Olga Popova/Shutterstock; p.5(right) Stephanie Reid; p.5(bottom) Nelson Marques/Shutterstock; p.6(left) Lee Aucoin; p.6(right) Arvind Balaraman/Shutterstock; p.7 USDA; p.8(top) Elena Schweitzer/Shutterstock; p.8(bottom) Dan Ionut Popescu/Shutterstock; p.8(insert) Sashkin/Shutterstock; p.9(middle background) Igor Shikov/Shutterstock; p.9(bottom) Shinya Sasaki/Getty Images; p.10(left) Arnold John Labrentz/Shutterstock; p.10(right) Larina Natalia/Shutterstock; p.11(top) Madlen/Shutterstock; p.11(left) Elena Elisseeva/Shutterstock; p.11(right) Marco Mayer/Shutterstock; p.12(bottom left) Imageman/Shutterstock; p.12(top right) Sevenke/Shutterstock; p.12(bottom right) Janet Faye Hastings/Shutterstock; p.13(top) Andrew Gentry/Shutterstock; p.13(bottom right) Photolibrary; p.14 AVAVA/Shutterstock; p.15(top left) Kenneth William Caleno/Shutterstock; p.15(top right) Julio Pelaez/MAXPPP/Newscom; p.15(bottom) James Anderson; p.16(top) Msheldrake/Shutterstock; p.16(bottom left) Sarsmis/Shutterstock; p.16(middle) Jiri Hera/Shutterstock; p.16(right) Oliver Hoffmann/Shutterstock; p.17(left) Stephanie Reid; p.17(left insert) Booka/Shutterstock; p.17(right) David M. Martin, M.D./Photo Researchers, Inc.; p.18 Linda Kloosterhof/iStockphoto; p.19(top left) James Anderson; p.19(bottom left) Piccianeri/Dreamstime; p.19(bottom right) Cathyclapper/Dreamstime; p.19(middle right) James Anderson; p.19(top right) Stephen Aaron Rees/Shutterstock; p.20 Shutterstock; p.20(bottom, left) DennisNata/Shutterstock; p.20(bottom right) James Anderson; p.21(top) Photolibrary; p.21(bottom) Mettus/Shutterstock; p.22(left) Elena Stepanova/Shutterstock; p.22(inset) Shutterstock; p.22(right) Kacso Sandor/Shutterstock; p.23(all) James Anderson; p.24 DUSAN ZIDAR/Shutterstock; p.25 Stephanie Frey/Shutterstock; p.26 Getty Images/Blend Images; p.27(top left) MANDEL NGAN; p.27(top right) Denis Tabler/Shutterstock; p.27(middle) IDAL/Shutterstock; p.27(bottom) Joao Virissimo/iStockphoto; p.28–29 Nicolle Rager Fuller; p.32(top) Newscom; p.32(bottom) Screwy/Shutterstock; Back cover Dusan Zidar/Shutterstock

Teacher Created Materials

5301 Oceanus Drive
Huntington Beach, CA 92649-1030
http://www.tcmpub.com
ISBN 978-1-4333-3088-9
Copyright © 2012 by Teacher Created Materials, Inc.
BP 5028

Table of Contents

Make It Yourself

Do you make your own meals? Chances are your parents cook most of your meals. But, you may know how to make some of the foods you like to eat. Are these foods healthy? Think about the food you eat and whether it is good for you. You only get one body. You may as well keep it healthy.

Start by making balanced meals that contain all the food groups. Grains and dairy are examples of food groups. So are protein, fruits, and vegetables. A balanced meal will give your body the energy and **nutrients** (NOO-tree-uhnts) it needs to make it through the day. It will also boost your brainpower. So make it healthy!

Fish is a great source of **protein** (PRO-teen).

Spinach is a great source of iron.

Whole-Grain Power

Some food products that you have at home may be made with whole grains. A whole grain is a cereal grain that still has its bran and germ. Bran helps to keep your heart and digestive system healthy. The germ is not like the germs that make you sick. The germ of a grain contains many vitamins and minerals that your body needs.

bran

endosperm

germ

Fuel Up!

Your days are busy! Food gives your body the fuel it needs to play and learn. When you feel hungry, your body is trying to tell you that you are running out of energy. Be sure to eat slowly and do not overeat. It takes 20 minutes for your body to tell your brain that it has had enough.

E 1/2 F

Planning Your Meals

It may be easy to open a bag of chips when you are hungry. That does not mean it is smart! Hunger can affect your thinking. Your body wants you to eat. But, you may not think about which foods are healthy. Having a plan can really help you choose wisely.

Create a list of **recipes** for meals and snacks that you like. The meals and snacks on your list should contain foods from as many food groups as possible. Then, hang your list on the refrigerator door. Choose something off the list when you are hungry and make it.

Making a list will help keep track of what you are eating. It will also help you notice how much you are eating. If you start eating a large bag of chips, you may just finish the entire bag. But, if you make a one-serving snack, all you will eat is one serving.

After-School Snack List

Monday	Tuesday	Wednesday	Thursday	Friday
•ants on a log	•cheese and crackers	•peanut butter and banana sandwich on whole wheat bread	•carrot sticks and hummus	•pumpkin seeds
•glass of milk	•apple			•raisins
				•string cheese

Create a list of after-school snacks that you can make yourself and hang it on your refrigerator.

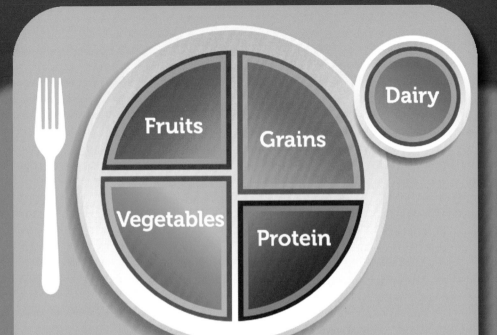

Choose**MyPlate**.gov

Choose MyPlate

It can be easy to make healthy food choices. Using the MyPlate guide is a great place to start. Go to **www.choosemyplate.gov** for some great tips and ideas about healthy eating.

Ready, Set, Cook!

Before you can start cooking, you need to ask for permission. It is best to ask an adult for help at first. You also need to know some basic rules. Cooking and preparing food can be dangerous. You may need knives to cut your food. The stove you use to cook is hot and could burn you. Also, some raw foods have dangerous **bacteria**.

Did You Know?

Raw meat can have bacteria, such as **salmonella** (sal-muh-NEL-uh), that can be harmful to humans. Be sure to cook meat to the proper temperature shown on the package. Check a cookbook if it is not listed.

salmonella

Food Safety Rules

These rules will keep you from getting sick or hurt when you make meals:

1. First, wash your hands with warm, soapy water.
2. Do not put cooked food on a plate that had raw meats or eggs on it. And do not lick your fingers or mixing spoons when cooking with raw meats or eggs.
3. Make sure you use potholders when you take things out of a hot oven.
4. Never leave your food while it is cooking on a fire or stove.
5. Be careful with knives. Ask a grown-up to help you cut foods.

Cooking Essentials

All cooks need some basic tools. Here are a few that you may already have:

- ✔ measuring cup
- ✔ measuring spoons
- ✔ pots and pans
- ✔ knife (only use with a grown-up's help)
- ✔ cutting board
- ✔ spatula

How To Choose Healthy Ingredients

All meals and snacks you make have **ingredients**. To make healthy meals and snacks, we need healthy ingredients. The best ingredients are fresh. They include locally grown fruits and vegetables. They also include whole grains and lean protein. Lean protein includes fish, poultry, and beef that do not have a lot of fat in them.

Study the MyPlate guide. Look at all the types of foods you should be eating. Look at the correct proportions you need on your plate. Then plan your meals.

Asia and Eastern Africa— *Jackfruit* is the largest type of fruit that grows in trees. This fruit gives off a rotting smell when it is ripe. If you can get past the smell, you may find this fruit to be delicious. It can be eaten raw or cooked. It is even used in medicine!

Greece—*Greek yogurt* is thick and creamy and does not have the sugar that many other yogurts have. It strengthens your immune system and bones!

Here are a few tips to follow:

- ✔ Choose fresh foods that do not come in a box or a can.

- ✔ Go bold! Fruits and vegetables with the darkest, boldest colors are usually better for you. These include berries, sweet potatoes, and broccoli.

- ✔ Read the ingredients list. Some ingredients lists are full of words that are hard to read and say. That may be a sign that a food is loaded with unhealthy ingredients.

- ✔ Read the nutrition facts label. Look for foods with lots of **fiber** and protein. Find foods with lots of vitamins and minerals.

Japan—*Soybeans* are used in everything in Japan from soy sauce to tofu. They are full of protein and are good for your heart.

India—*Lentils* are eaten at least twice a day in most Indian homes. This legume is served with steamed rice or bread. Packed with vitamins and minerals, lentils have been shown to be good for the heart.

Making Healthy Meals

Making healthy meals for yourself does not have to be hard. It can be an easy and fun activity. Look at the foods in your kitchen and think about the types of meals you could make. Choose your ingredients and be creative. You can even make meals with your family and friends.

Energy Foods

Your body converts **carbohydrates** (kahr-boh-HI-dreyts) and starches into sugars that it can use for energy. These foods include rice, sweet potatoes, corn, oats, and barley.

brown rice

oats

sweet potato

Break It Down with Insulin

Insulin is a **hormone** that is produced in the body. It helps to regulate **metabolism** (muh-TAB-uh-liz-uhm). Insulin processes the sugars in cells so that they are converted into energy. Sometimes the body does not produce enough insulin. When this happens a person develops **diabetes** (dahy-uh-BEET-eez). People with diabetes have to check their blood sugar on a regular basis. If their blood sugar level is high, they inject themselves with insulin to help process the sugar.

A glucose meter tests blood sugar.

One good reason to make healthy meals is blood sugar. Healthy foods help to keep your blood sugar at normal levels. They will also keep you happy and full of energy. Have you ever had a headache when you are really hungry? Or, maybe you felt like you were in a bad mood. It might be because of low blood sugar.

Blood sugar, or **blood glucose** (GLOO-kohs) as it is also known, is sugar that is carried by your blood through your body. This sugar is not like the sugar cane that you cook with. It is the sugars your body gets from the foods you eat. These sugars give your cells energy. This energy is used to power your body. This energy does not last forever. Your body uses it up. Then you have low blood sugar. Your cells do not have as much energy. You may feel tired. Your brain may not be as quick. That is when you must eat.

Fuel Up with Breakfast

Breakfast may just be the most important meal of the day. Why? Before breakfast, you are sleeping. You have not eaten for many hours. You may have low blood sugar when you wake up. Your body is hungry. You need energy to start your day off right.

A healthy breakfast can help wake your body and mind. It can give you the energy to walk or ride your bike to school. It can give you the power to lift your backpack. A healthy breakfast can even help your brain. That will allow you to do better in school.

Breakfast can be quick to make. It can be delicious, too. Fruit, whole grains, and low-fat protein are your best bets. They will give your brain a boost and your body what it needs to get your busy day off to a great start!

Colorful Eggs

You may have seen eggs that are brown or white. But, have you ever seen a chicken lay an egg that was blue or green? It can happen. Chickens that lay these different colored eggs have the blue egg gene. This unusual trait is passed down from the chicken's parents.

Play-with-Your-Vegetables Breakfast Muffin

Ingredients

- nonstick cooking spray
- 1 egg
- $\frac{1}{4}$ cup shredded, low-fat or part-skim cheese (any kind)
- $\frac{1}{2}$ whole wheat English muffin
- $\frac{1}{4}$ cup of your favorite vegetables, diced (bell pepper, spinach, etc.)
- your favorite whole fruit (grapes, strawberries, banana, plum, etc.)

Directions

1. Toast the English muffin half.
2. Spray a large microwave-safe mug with nonstick cooking spray.
3. Add the egg to the mug. Then add the cheese and your favorite vegetables.
4. Stir or whip with fork.
5. Microwave the mug on high for 35-45 seconds.
6. Carefully remove the eggs from the mug and let it stand for about 2 minutes.
7. Add your favorite fruit to the plate.
8. Put the egg, cheese, and vegetable mixture on top of the English muffin and enjoy.

Serves 1; Nutrition Facts (approximate): **Calories** 343; Sodium 517 mg; Carbohydrate 47 g; Fiber 6 g; Protein 37 g; Sugar 20 g; Fat 11g

Punch Up Your Lunch!

Tired of having the same lunch day after day? Is your stomach growling by noon? Start packing a lunch with punch! A lunch with whole grains, vegetables, and low-fat protein will help you put an end to your hunger. It will also quiet your stomach.

Tired of sandwiches for lunch? Wraps are a great option. They are fun to make and easy to eat. Start your wrap with whole-grain tortillas. Use whatever low-fat cheese and deli meat you like. Be sure to add some crunchy vegetables! Do not forget to pack a piece of fruit, too.

TURKEY ROLL 'EM

Ingredients

- 2 teaspoons Dijon honey mustard
- 1 8-inch fat-free or whole-grain wheat tortilla
- 1 slice reduced-fat cheese
- 2 slices fat-free turkey breast
- $\frac{1}{4}$ cup shredded carrot
- 2 lettuce or spinach leaves, washed and torn into bite-size pieces

Directions

1. Spread mustard over tortilla.
2. Top with cheese, turkey, carrot, and lettuce.
3. Roll up tortilla. Cut in half (ask a grown-up to help).

Serves 1; Nutrition Facts (approximate):
Calories 184; Total Fat 3 g; Sodium 774 mg; Carbohydrate 25 g; Fiber 4 g; Protein 15 g

Your stomach is part of your **digestive** (di-JES-tiv) **system**. This system is made of the organs and tissues that process the food you eat. When your stomach is empty, your digestive system begins to contract, or flex. This pushes air and stomach juices around. Any food that is left is picked up. These juices make a gurgling and rumbling sound. It can sound like a growl! This noise means you need food.

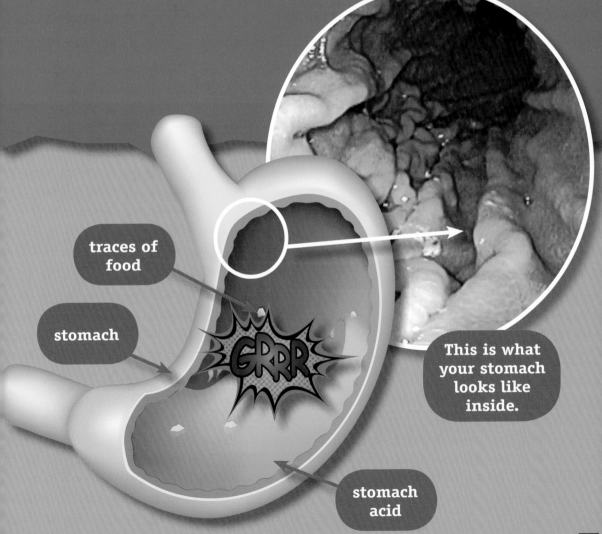

traces of food

stomach

GRRR

This is what your stomach looks like inside.

stomach acid

Eat a Balanced Dinner

Dinnertime is the perfect time for you to help out in the kitchen. Have your parents ever made something for dinner that you did not like? Well, help them out! They may let you decide what to eat if you offer to help cook. They may learn more about what you like to eat. You may learn something about your family, too.

Protein Power

Protein is a good addition to any meal. Protein helps build up your muscles and keeps you from getting sick and hungry. It can be found in meat, nuts, beans, and dairy.

If your parents make the main dish, ask if you can make a side dish or two. Side dishes can be easy to make—and can taste great. Some of them do not even need to be cooked.

Pizza Salad Stack

Ingredients

- 8 tomato slices
- 8 low-fat mozzarella slices
- 8 basil leaves
- 8 slices of mushroom

- olive oil
- balsamic vinegar
- $\frac{1}{4}$ cup of sliced black olives

Directions

1. Place the 8 slices of tomato on a plate.
2. Top each slice of tomato with a slice of mozzarella, mushroom, and one basil leaf.
3. Drizzle a small amount of olive oil and balsamic vinegar over each stack.
4. Sprinkle the sliced black olives over the top and serve.

Serves 4; Nutrition Facts (approximate for 1 serving): Calories 51; Total Fat 3.5 g; Sodium 100 mg; Carbohydrate 2 g; Fiber 2 g; Protein 4 g

Snack Attack

"If you eat now, it will ruin your dinner!" Sound familiar? Maybe you have been told not to snack between meals. But the truth is, it is good to have small meals and one or two healthy snacks during the day. Everything you do—playing, learning, sports—takes energy. So it is a good idea to refuel when you get hungry. Just make sure you do not eat too much. You do want to be hungry at mealtimes.

Do you love sushi? Maybe you have never tried it. Make your own "sushi" with this fun recipe. If you are really daring, try eating your sushi with chopsticks! This dessert recipe is not real sushi, but it is a fun imitation of it.

Banzai Banana Berry Sushi

Ingredients
- 1 8-inch whole-wheat tortilla
- 2 tablespoons peanut butter
- 1 banana
- 1 tablespoon honey
- 2 strawberries, sliced

Serves 1; Nutrition Facts (approximate): Calories 470; Total Fat 17 g; Sodium 327 mg; Carbohydrate 86 g; Fiber 10 g; Protein 13 g; Sugar 40 g

Directions
1. Spread a thin layer of peanut butter across the tortilla. Stop when you get about $\frac{1}{4}$-inch from the edge.
2. Peel banana and put it in the middle of the tortilla. (It is okay if it breaks or gets a little mushy.)
3. Roll up the tortilla tightly. Put it seam-side down on a plate.
4. Have a grown-up help you cut it into about 8 pieces. Drizzle honey across the top in a zigzag pattern.
5. Place a slice of strawberry on top of each piece.

Raw Fish?

Most sushi is raw fish with rice. The fish used for sushi has to be fresh because it is raw. When we cook meat, the heat kills any bacteria on the meat that could harm us. However, raw meat may still have some bacteria. That is why the fish used in sushi must be very fresh and well-cleaned.

Taste Bud Trivia

The next time you take a bite of food, think about how it tastes. And then, thank your **taste buds**! Those little bumps on your tongue help you taste foods that are sweet, salty, sour, and bitter. Imagine if a lemon and a scoop of chocolate ice cream tasted the same. Or, imagine if your favorite food had no taste at all.

Chemicals in your food make your taste buds work. Taste buds are really tiny nerve endings. Each person has about 10,000 of them! They send messages to the brain when you eat something. Those messages tell the brain that ice cream is sweet and a lemon is sour. There are four basic tastes: sweet, salty, sour, and bitter.

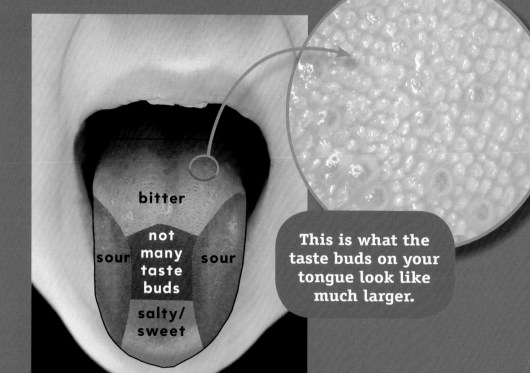

bitter

sour

not many taste buds

sour

salty/ sweet

This is what the taste buds on your tongue look like much larger.

Ready-made and fast foods are packed with fat and salt. This may excite your taste buds—but it is not good for your body. When it comes to snack time, look for healthier options that are just as fast.

Eight Is Enough

Ingredients

- 8 whole-wheat crackers
- 3 slices low-fat ham or turkey, cut into 8 squares that fit on the crackers
- 2 low-fat cheese slices, cut into 8 squares
- $\frac{1}{2}$ small cucumber, cut into 8 slices
- Hummus or low-fat ranch dressing (optional)

Directions

1. Put cucumber slices in a separate small plastic bag or container.
2. Place crackers, cheese, and meat in a container.
3. When it is time for a snack, place one meat and cheese square on each cracker and top with a cucumber slice. Enjoy!

Optional: Dip into hummus or low-fat ranch dressing.

Serves 1; Nutrition Facts (approximate):
Calories 364 ; Total Fat 11 g; Sodium 741 mg; Carbohydrate 33 g; Fiber 5 g; Protein 34 g

Snack on Fruits and Vegetables

Why does food on a stick seem to taste better? Well, maybe it does not really taste better, but it is sure fun to eat and make. You can choose all kinds of foods to put on a stick. The best kinds may be fruits. Have a grown-up help you cut the fruit into bite-sized pieces. Watch out for the pointy ends of the skewers!

Smooth Sailing

Do you have a blender and a variety of your favorite fruits and vegetables? Smoothies are a great way to get more fruits and vegetables into your diet. You can blend together any type of fruit, juices, or yogurt you have in the house. Get creative! Keep trying different combinations and come up with your own special blend!

Rainbow Kabobs

Ingredients

- 1 kiwi, cut into 4 chunks
- 4 small strawberries
- 4 pineapple chunks
- $\frac{1}{4}$ mango, cut into 4 chunks
- 2 skewers or 4 plastic coffee stirrers
- low-fat yogurt (optional)

Directions

1. Push a skewer or coffee stirrer through a strawberry. Slide the strawberry to the other end of the skewer.
2. Do the same with a pineapple, kiwi, and mango.
3. Repeat so that you have eight pieces of fruit on each skewer. If using coffee stirrers, put four pieces on each one.

Optional: Dip fruit in low-fat yogurt as you eat it!

Serves 1; Nutrition Facts (approximate):
Calories 173; Sodium 5 mg; Carbohydrate 50 g; Fiber 3.5 g; Protein 3 g; Sugar 33 g

Take Charge in the Kitchen!

You may not need to cook for yourself all of the time. But, you do have the power to make healthy meals and snacks when you need to. You can start small and help your parents prepare meals. This can make each meal a family event.

Eating smart takes some planning. Find some recipes in this book you would like to try. Or, find other recipes on the Internet. Then, make a grocery list of the foods you need. Check the nutrition labels as you shop. Before you know it, you will have a list of healthy recipes that are fun to make and fun to eat. Pretty soon, the kitchen may be your favorite room in the house!

It has been shown that families that eat together are healthier and happier.

From the White House to Your House

First Lady Michelle Obama is making it her mission to get kids to live healthy lives. Her recipe? Eat more fruits, vegetables, and whole grains. And, be active for at least 60 minutes a day!

Fast Food Craze

Fast food can be okay when you are in a rush. Not all of the food on the menu is healthy, however. Luckily, fast food chains have nutrition facts posted about their food that you can check. This can help you make good food choices while on the go.

Lab: Start a School Garden

Nothing tastes better than fruits and vegetables you grow yourself. Even First Lady Michelle Obama planted a vegetable garden at the White House. Now, school gardens are sprouting up all over the country!

Materials

- fruit seeds
- vegetable seeds
- plant food
- drawing paper
- crayons and markers
- gardening tools

Procedure:

1. Work with your teacher and class to find space on your school campus that would be a good spot for a school garden. It does not have to be big, but it does need to get a lot of sunlight. Make sure there is a water source nearby.

2. Have your teacher or your whole class meet with your school principal to get permission.

3. Talk to your parents to see if they can help. Try to get a group of parents together who can help get the garden started and maintain it. See if other teachers and classes want to get involved, too.

4. Decide what you want to grow. Will it be fruits and vegetables to eat at school? Do you want to supply the cafeteria with fresh produce? Or would you like to start with a small herb garden?

5. Look up information about what kinds of plants grow best in your climate. Find out how much care they need.

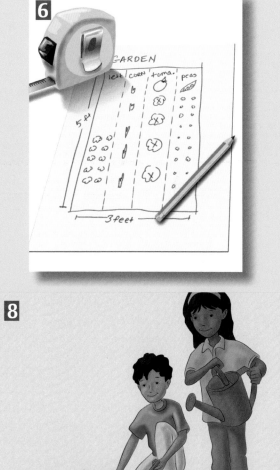

6. Measure the size of the area you will use. Draw a picture to figure out how you will plot your garden.

7. Ask for donations or plan a fundraiser to raise money for seeds, plant food, gardening tools, and any other supplies you might need to get started.

8. Plant your garden and help it grow!

Glossary

bacteria—a single-celled organism that can be found on and in our bodies; some types are good for us, while others are harmful

blood glucose—a sugar that is carried by blood through the body; a sugar the body uses for energy

calories— units of energy that that tell you how much energy you can receive from foods and drinks

carbohydrates—sugars that the body can use as energy

diabetes—a disease that affects how the body uses sugar

digestive system—a system of the body the changes food into energy and waste

fiber—part of fruits, vegetables, and grains that keeps your intestines working

hormone— a chemical in the body that tells it how to work and grow

ingredients—foods that are parts of a meal

insulin—a hormone that converts sugars from foods into energy

metabolism—all of the processes that provide the body energy to work

nutrients—chemicals your body uses to live and grow or a substance that helps your metabolism

protein— a substance found in meat, beans, and nuts that helps build up the tissues in your body

recipes—instructions for making or preparing meals and snacks

salmonella—a type of bacteria that can contaminate food and cause illness in mammals

taste buds—small nerves on the tongue that allow us to taste

Index

Making School Lunches Healthier

Jamie Oliver is a celebrity chef. But his top goal is to teach kids and families how to eat healthy.

He has made headlines by going to public schools and taking over their kitchens. He found that many schools were serving unhealthy meals to students. He brought in fresh fruits and vegetables. He got rid of fried foods. He replaced sugary drinks with water and milk. He worked with the kitchen staff to make great-tasting, healthy food. The kids loved it! He even went into people's homes. He showed them easy ways to cook healthy meals for their families.

It takes a lot of work to get people to accept new ways to eat. But Jamie Oliver is on a mission to make us healthier!

Personal Challenge

Next time you are in the grocery store, choose one fruit and one vegetable that you have never tried before. If you are not sure how to eat it, check out some recipes online. You might just find a new favorite food!